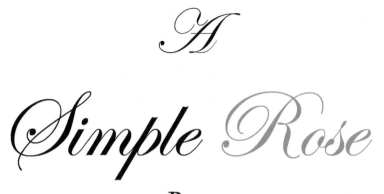

A Simple Rose

By
K. Y. Baker

Illustration
Allison Bennett

ISBN 978-1-944245-39-9

"*Something as simple as a rose may leave a lasting impression on the heart.*"

– K. Y. Baker

Mrs. Washington's class was one of the best 3rd grade classes in the school. They knew their multiplication as well as division.

Mrs. Washington was bilingual; she could speak more than one language well. Her students were taught how to speak Spanish.

Her class was fun to be in especially during the holidays. She would give a party for Halloween, Thanksgiving, and Christmas. She would even make up a special day to have a party for the students doing their work well.

Every party would be better than the last, but one of her students never had any fun. The student name was Addison.

Addison was an intelligent little girl, but she didn't have any friends. The reason is because of her leg. Her left leg was a prosthetic leg which is a false leg.

At the beginning of the school year, Mrs. Washington explained to her class about Addison's leg, but it didn't matter. The boys and girls still picked on her, and Mrs. Washington didn't notice.

The students didn't get behind her in line or sat next to her in the cafeteria. When the class would go to recess, Addison would play on the swings alone. Sometimes four girls would walk towards her and bully her.

"Hey no legs" said Ella.

"How many times do you have to keep saying that? I have legs and I can move just like all of you", said Addison.

"Get up then." Tea said, while folding her arms.

"You all have seen me walk before and I'm tired of this, it's a new year" Addison explained as she held back her tears.

"I don't care what year it is. You're still ugly and have no legs" said Rebekah.

"How do you even walk with that thing?" asked Nichole.

"You can see, you have glasses" said Addison.

"Just shut-up" Ella said as she pushed her out the swing.

The four girls laughed as she fell back onto the cold ground. She didn't get up until they walked away. She wanted to cry because she couldn't believe they were still bullying her, and it's almost February.

Addison was glad that the weekend had finally come. She didn't have to deal with the children for two days. She could go to her doctor's appointment on Saturday and have peace.

Saturday was finally here! Addison was looking forward to her appointment. She gets to practice her balance and coordination. She also does other types of exercises for her leg and body.

While she was doing her exercises with her doctor, she noticed a boy from her school in the hallway looking at her. She felt uncomfortable because she didn't want to be teased on the weekend.

Dr. Jenkins noticed her smile had disappeared, so he turned his head towards the doorway. He saw the boy and gave him a look that made him move along.

Addison smiled and continued to do her exercises.

"Sunday came and went", Addison thought to herself as she walked into the classroom.

Once she sat in her seat, she saw Mrs. Stevens talking to Mrs. Washington and the boy from this past weekend standing next to them.

The bell buzzed and Mrs. Stevens left without the boy. Mrs. Washington closes the door and stood in front of the class to introduce him. "Boys and girls, this is Greg Jenkins. He was in Mrs. Stevens' class, but now he is joining our amazing 3rd grade class. Have a seat at an empty desk."

Addison watched the boy as he sat down. All she could think about was how he was going to tease her.

When P.E. time came, Greg noticed Addison moved to the back of the line. He saw that no one wanted to sit next to her at lunch. During recess, he saw her on the swings alone with her head down.

The school day was done, and Greg walked home. When he arrived, he said hello to his mother and went to his dad's office.

"Daddy, can I ask you something?" Greg asked.

"You can talk to me about anything." Dad answered.

"The girl you were working with Saturday doesn't have any friends", said Greg.

"Addison Jones, how do you know?" Dad asked.

"I'm in her class now, because you and mom asked for me to switch", said Greg.

"Correct, Mrs. Washington has an advance class", explained Dad.

"I understand, but what is wrong with that girl?" Greg asked.

"Why do you think something is wrong with her?" Greg's dad asked.

"No one wants to be near her", said Greg.

"Nothing is wrong with her; I think her classmates don't understand why she has to have that leg. And from the look upon your face last weekend you don't either", Dad said.

"Can you explain it to me?" asked Greg.

"Sure, her leg didn't fully develop when she was born, so we had to remove it once she got a little older. Then we replaced it with a prosthetic leg. She comes to me in order to help her use her prosthetic leg like it is her own", Dad said.

After Greg's dad explained why Addison has a fake leg, he then gave him a book that could also help him understand.

Greg looks at the pictures and read a little. He then realized she was not different from anybody else.

The next day in Mrs. Washington's class, she talked to them about "Black History Month" and the Valentine's Day party.

While Mrs. Washington was teaching history, Addison was dreading the party. Ever since she was in the 1st grade, she has always given her classmates something, but she never received anything from them for Valentine's Day.

As the week went by Addison would look in the mirror and say,

"Nothing is wrong with me. I am just like everybody else. I will not allow others to keep stealing my joy. I can kick a ball like Jessica and run faster than anybody in my class. I am amazing, but why can't they see?"

Addison's mom and dad took her to the store to purchase some Valentine's Day treats for her classmates. Her dad saw tears in her eyes while she put the candy in the basket.

"Baby girl, what's wrong?" her dad asked.

"I don't want to pass out any treats because no one will give me anything", Addison explained.

"Your mother and I never once taught you eye for an eye. You treat others how you want to be treated. You may be in 3rd grade, but you are very bright. Don't allow them to change that."

"Can I just stay home?" Addison asked with tears in her eyes.

"You have to learn to ignore their words, because they are just words. There is no truth to what they speak. Just know that everything will be all right and you can do all things through Christ who strengthens you."

Addison hugs her daddy, but still felt sad.

The Valentine's Day party has finally arrived. Addison was sitting in class with all her candy and she saw a lot of kids with their big bags. She was hoping that someone would give her something.

Mrs. Washington told the class to put their bags to the side because they will pass out candy before recess.

Addison's heart was beating fast all day. She believed everything her daddy told her, but she still wanted something from a classmate.

After lunch, the class came back to the room with smiles on their faces because they couldn't wait to pass out their treats.

Once the class settled down, Mrs. Washington walked towards her desk to get her clipboard with all her students' names.

She called the students in alphabetical order to pass out their candy. She noticed the first six students didn't give Addison anything.

She called Greg Jenkins to pass out his treats. He told the teacher his mother will bring them to class later. Then she called Addison Jones.

Addison passed out her treats and one student whispered to another, "If we eat this we may lose our legs."

Addison over heard what the student said, but continued to pass out her candy.

Once she finished, she sat down, and wiped her tears. The teacher saw and gave her some candy. Then she continued to call the rest.

Addison looked around and saw everyone had a lot of candy and cards, but not her. She felt so sad, and tried her best not to show it.

Greg's mother came into the classroom with goodie bags for the students. Mrs. Washington told Greg he could pass them out.

Greg started to pass out goodie bags. Inside the bags were candy, crayons, coloring books, stickers, pencils, and Valentine's Day cards.

The students couldn't believe how much stuff was in their bag, but there was one bag left on the teacher's table and it had a rose in it.

Greg made sure that would be the last bag he passed out. One student asked, "Who bag is that?" Greg smiled, grabbed the bag and gave it to Addison.

Addison didn't say anything, but looked at him. Greg told her to read the card, and then he went back to his seat to eat his candy.

Recess was finally here and Addison ran outside with the rose in her hand. She sat in a swing with a smile on her face. Greg was about to walk towards her, but two girls and two boys stopped him.

"Why did you give her a rose?" Ella asked.

"You know you will catch the no leg disease. My cousin told me about it", said Levi.

"There is no such thing and she is just like you and me." Greg explained

"No she isn't, she has no legs," said Rebekah

"Yes, she does. The other leg is just a fake. You all are mean and nothing good will happen to mean people." Greg said as he walked towards Addison.

Greg sat in the swing next to Addison and smiled at her.

"No one, besides my parents has ever given me anything on Valentine's Day. Thank You!" Addison said.

"You're welcome." said Greg.

The two stayed on the swings until recess was over. Ever since Valentine's Day, Addison had someone to talk to, and the others started to come around when they saw nothing happen to Greg.

No matter how many people started talking to her, she will always consider Greg as her best friend. If you ever ask Addison how she and Greg became friends? She will always say, "It started with a simple rose."

"*I Got A Rose*"

By K.Y. Baker

I got a rose today from a boy I like.

His smile is as warm as a fire burning in a fireplace in the winter.

His aroma made me close my eyes to think of Sunday dinner; Collard greens, macaroni and cheese, cornbread and black eyed peas.

I got a rose today from a boy I like.
His skin was as bright as the sun. Even if it was dark as the night, it didn't matter.
The skin tone is not what stole my eyes.

The personality is what kidnapped them-it was as sweet as a honeysuckle.

Can you believe that a simple rose
from a boy who walks with his chest out and head held up to the heavens
made my day fill complete?

No bling or folding of paper;
Nothing for my back or my feet-
Just a simple rose from a confident guy.

I got a rose today from a boy I like.
It made my day complete.
It made it feel larger than life.
It was simple, but it will last longer than anything.

I got a rose today.

CPSIA information can be obtained at www.ICGtesting.com
Printed in the USA
BVOW10*1850060116

431502BV00023B/34/P

9 781944 245399